COMMUNITY WORKERS

A Police Officer's Job

VIRGINIA O'BRIAN

Cavendish
Square

New York

Published in 2015 by Cavendish Square Publishing, LLC
243 5th Avenue, Suite 136, New York, NY 10016

Copyright © 2015 by Cavendish Square Publishing, LLC

First Edition

CPSIA Compliance Information: Batch #WS14CSQ

All websites were available and accurate when this book was sent to press.

Library of Congress Cataloging-in-Publication Data

O'Brian, Virginia.
A police officer's job / Virginia O'Brian.
pages cm. — (Community workers)
Includes index.
ISBN 978-1-62712-361-7 (hardcover) ISBN 978-1-62712-363-1 (paperback) ISBN 978-1-62712-364-8 (ebook)
1. Police—Juvenile literature. I. Title.

HV7922.O27 2015
363.2023—dc23

2014001535

Editorial Director: Dean Miller
Editor: Amy Hayes
Copy Editor: Cynthia Roby
Art Director: Jeffrey Talbot
Designer: Douglas Brooks
Photo Researcher: J8 Media
Production Manager: Jennifer Ryder-Talbot
Production Editor: David McNamara

The photographs in this book are used by permission and through the courtesy of: Cover photo by Darrin Klimek/Digital Vision/Thinkstock; Darrin Klimek/Digital Vision/Thinkstock, 5; fStop/SuperStock, 7; Visions of America/SuperStock, 9; benkrut/iStock Editorial/Thinkstock, 11; Jupiterimages/Stockbyte/Thinkstock, 13; Egon Bömsch/imagebrok/imagebroker.net/SuperStock, 15; Andrew Olscher/Shutterstock.com, 17; Chris Maddaloni/Contributor/CQ-Roll Call Group/Getty Images, 19; UpperCut Images/SuperStock, 21.

Printed in the United States of America

Contents

We are **police officers**.

We help people.

We keep people safe.

We start our day at the **police station.**

We find out where we will **patrol** that day.

I patrol the roads. I make sure people don't break the **law**.

I have to write a **ticket** if a person drives too fast.

We patrol on horses.

There's a big **parade** today.

We make sure that people march safely.

Sometimes we patrol on a boat.

We make sure that everyone in the water is being safe.

13

We patrol on bikes.

We ride our bikes through the park.

We make sure everyone in the park is safe.

15

I work in the street.

I use my hands to tell drivers
when to stop and go.

I make sure people cross
the street safely.

I patrol with Vandy.

Vandy is a police dog.

Vandy helps me look for **clues**.

Sometimes I stop and talk to people.

They thank me for keeping them safe.

I'm happy to help them!

Words to Know

clues (**klooz**) things that help police solve a mystery

law (**law**) a rule that people must follow

parade (puh-**rayd**) a group of people that march together down a street

patrol (puh-**trol**) to walk or ride around an area to make sure people are safe

police officers (po-**lees aw**-fih-sirz) people who make sure others are safe and follow laws

police station (po-**lees stay**-shen) a place where police officers work

ticket (**tih**-kit) something given to a driver who breaks the law

Find Out More

Books

Jobs People Do: A Day in the Life of a Police Officer
by Linda Hayward, DK Publishing

Officer Buckle and Gloria
by Peggy Rathman, Putnam Juvenile

Police Officers on Patrol
by Kersten Hamilton, Viking Juvenile

Website

Community Club: Police Officer
teacher.scholastic.com/commclub/officer/

Index